Your friend, **Jimmy!**

Count on Golf

by Susan Greene

Illustrations by Margaret L. Rose

Excel Publishing
Troy, Michigan

For my Mom and Dad, parents I could always count on!
S.G.

For my beautiful little "Sweet Peas," Caitlin and Colleen.
My love always. M.R.

Text and illustrations copyright © 1998 Susan Greene

First Edition 1998
Published by Excel Publishing

Library of Congress Catalog Card Number: 98-93113

International Standard Book Number 0-9651100-9-5

Printed in Singapore

10 9 8 7 6 5 4 3

"I'm golfing in a tournament today,
And now I must get ready to play.

Help me prepare all that I need.
Turn the page and we will procccd."

 **is for one putter.**

"I'll add ONE putter to my bag,

Hoping to sink all putts and never lag."

**2**
is for two
golf shoes.

"I'll put **two** golf shoes on my feet.

Soft spikes really can't be beat!"

 **is for three**

gloves.

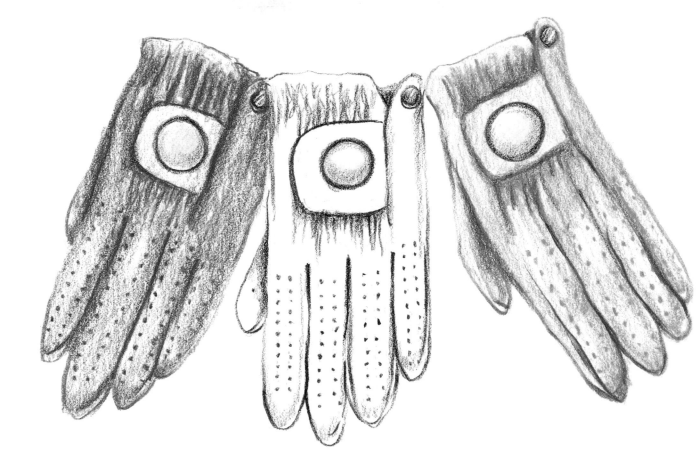

"I'll take **three** gloves so I have plenty to spare.

That gives me two extras and one to wear!"

 **is for four**

players.

"Each team has **four** players,
A foursome, they say.
And these are my partners,
My team for today."

 **5**  is for five

metal woods.

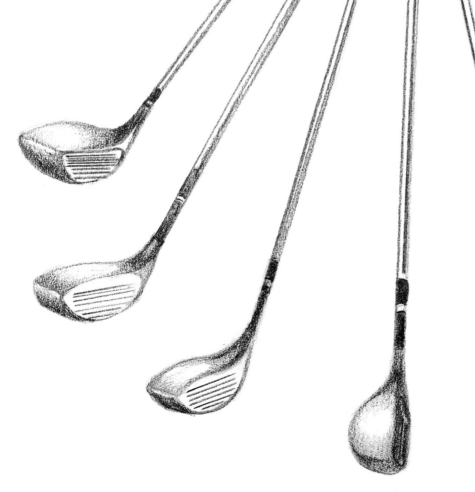

"**Five** metal woods are my next addition.

More equipment to help in my mission!"

 **is for six**

balls.

"I'll pack **six** balls for an ample supply.

I'll hit some low and hit some high!"

7 is for seven tees.
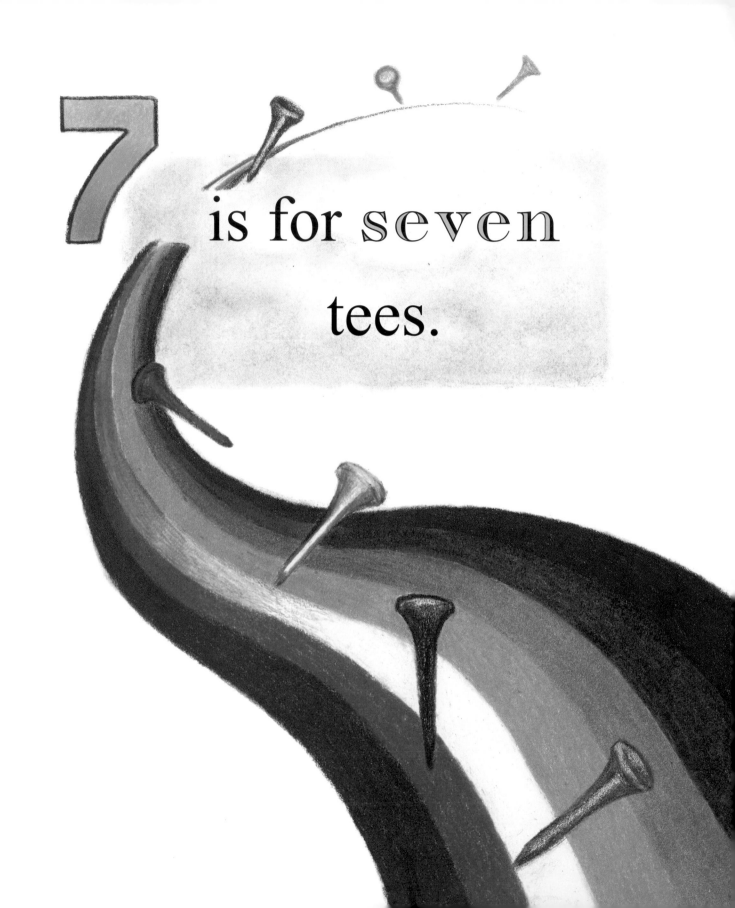

"I'll take SEVEN tees for the day.

You can see I've quite an array!"

8 is for eight irons.

"I'll add eight irons to the rest.

More help to win this golf contest!"

9 is for nine holes.

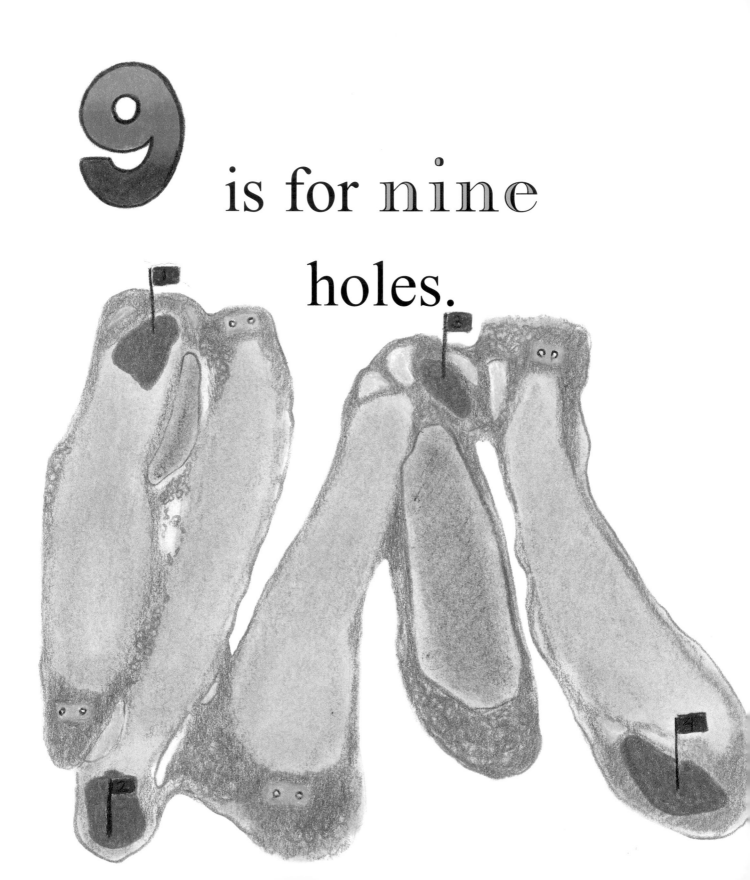

"Now I'm all packed and ready to play,
Nine holes of golf on the course today!

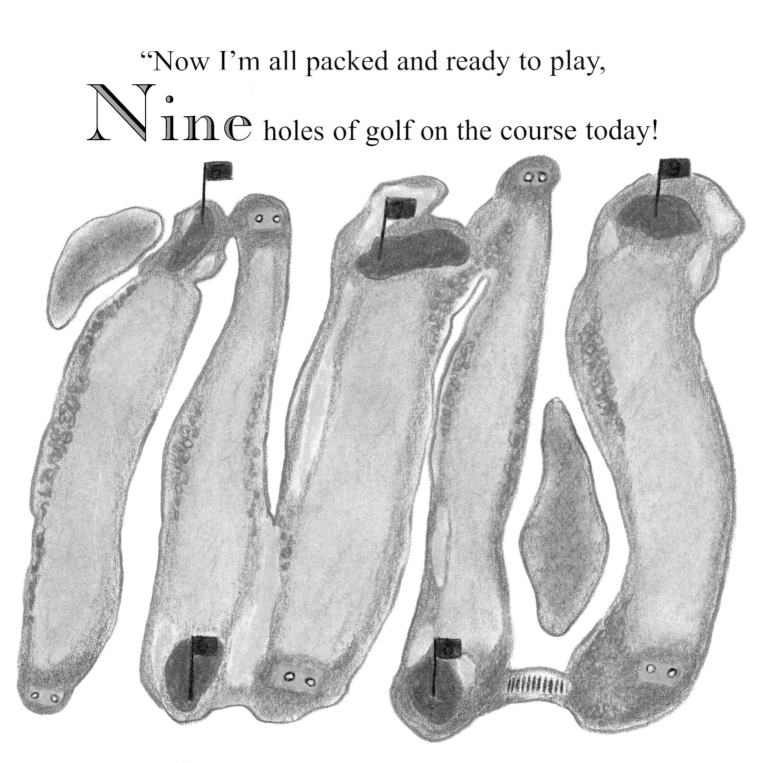

The nine-hole tournament will soon begin,
And I think we have a chance to win!"

10 is for ten trophies.

"There are **ten** trophies to be won,
But what's more important is having **FUN!**"

"When the tournament came to an end,
We did more than just contend.
Our talent proved to be supreme,
And we became the winning team!"

Count on Golf is so much fun,

How many putters do you see?

How many golf shoes do you see?

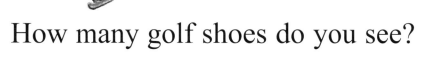

How many gloves do you see?

How many players do you see?

How many metal woods do you see?

But you must review before you're done!

How many balls do you see?

How many tees do you see?

How many irons do you see?

How many golf holes do you see?

How many trophies do you see?